SWEET & FRUITFUL

A Devotional Collection for Women

JULIA BETTENCOURT

All Scripture quotations are from the King James Bible.

The devotionals within this collection were previously
published to www.juliabettencourt.com

DEDICATION

This book is dedicated to my husband, who puts up
with me, even on days when I'm not too sweet.

CONTENTS

INTRODUCTION

As Christian women, we need to bear the sweet fruit that comes only from the Holy Spirit. We shouldn't be yielding fruit that is puny on the vines. Nor should we be missing fruit from the vines. The fruit we bear shouldn't be rotten, tasteless, or full of bugs either.

I trust this collection of devotionals will encourage you on your journey to bear that sweet Fruit of the Spirit. We have to be diligent in what we think, what we do, and what we say. Life for a Christian is all about living in the Spirit.

If we live in the Spirit, let us also walk in the Spirit. Galatians 5:25

PROVISIONS

But put ye on the Lord Jesus Christ, and
make not provision for the flesh, to fulfil
the lusts thereof. Romans 13:14

Making provisions is a fantastic thing when it comes to the necessities of life. Those who harvest and can vegetables and fruits or pack them away into the freezer are making provision for later down the road.

Isn't it just delightful to unscrew that ring on a home-jarred can of green beans in the middle of winter and pop that seal? Mmmm! Those beans taste just like they've been freshly picked off of the vine.

Putting away provisions is a wonderful concept, but I wonder how many of us put away things on the shelves of our lives that we shouldn't. That verse in Romans warns us, but how many of us heed it?

...and make not provision for the flesh... Romans 13:14

There are things we pack away in our canning jars, as it were, that can only lead to broken fellowship with Christ.

Negative Thoughts

What about all those negative thoughts that we get a good crop of and put up into our jars? It could be negative thoughts about our pastor, church, coworkers, or even our family members.

Casting down imaginations, and every high thing that exalteth itself against the knowledge of God, and bringing into captivity every thought to the obedience of Christ; 2 Corinthians 10:5

Negative Actions

Sometimes we do things that are nothing more than setting ourselves up for sin. Remember how David took Bathsheba's husband, Uriah, and put him at the front of the lines? (2 Samuel 11:15)

David made provision for Uriah to be killed so that he could have Bathsheba for himself. We have got to be aware of our actions.

For those of us that know Christ as Savior, our actions should be that of obedient children.

As obedient children, not fashioning yourselves
according to the former lusts in your ignorance:
But as he which hath called you is holy, so be ye
holy in all manner of conversation; Because it
is written, Be ye holy; for I am holy. 1 Peter 1:14-16

Envy

Look how David made this his provision for sin. (2 Samuel 11:2-27) He saw Bathsheba and wanted her. When he opened that jar of envy up, he only invited misery into his life.

Talk about opening a can of worms! Envy is listed right up there with the works of the flesh in Galatians.

Envyings, murders, drunkenness, revellings,
and such like: of the which I tell you before,
as I have also told you in time past, that
they which do such things shall not inherit
the kingdom of God. Galatians 5:21

Worry

Worries we jar up one jar at a time, never too many at once. At least that is how it is at first. Ever notice, however; that when we open them up later, we usually end up opening all the jars of worry at one time and devouring them all at once?

Be careful for nothing; but in every thing by
prayer and supplication with thanksgiving let
your requests be made known unto God. And the
peace of God, which passeth all understanding,
shall keep your hearts and minds through
Christ Jesus. Philippians 4:6-7

Pride

We can certainly pack this one away. Can't we? Some of us have several jars of pride lining the shelves of our lives. We don't always label it "pride" though.

We mark it neatly as "knowledge, "talent", or "spiritual growth". Not that there is anything wrong with those things, but sometimes we use them as excuses in order to justify our prideful attitudes.

When pride cometh, then cometh shame: but
with the lowly is wisdom. Proverbs 11:2

Time

Setting aside time is not a bad thing, but when we set it aside and put ourselves in situations where we are prone to sin it is. Many of us set aside time every week to sit down and watch a television show or two that we know doesn't honor God.

Some people set aside time to roam around on the internet to places that are not fit for a Christian. Some of us even set aside time to sit and gossip on the phone. In the end it makes provision for the flesh for us to sin.

See then that ye walk circumspectly, not as
fools, but as wise, Redeeming the time,
because the days are evil. Ephesians 5:15-16

Final Thoughts

When we are making provision for the flesh to rule our lives, we aren't giving the Spirit any leeway to develop that fruit we should be exhibiting. That's what we should be jarring up and lining our pantry shelves with...*The Fruit of the Spirit.*

When we go back to the verse we started with in Romans 13:14, it tells us how to avoid making provision for the flesh. We are to put on Christ!

But put ye on the Lord Jesus Christ, and
make not provision for the flesh, to fulfil
the lusts thereof. Romans 13:14

When we are putting on Christ in our daily lives, we are allowing the Spirit free reign and our fruit and the things we pack away will reflect that. These are the types of fruit we should exhibit.

Love	Joy	Peace
Longsuffering	Gentleness	Goodness
Faith	Meekness	Temperance

But the fruit of the Spirit is love, joy, peace,
longsuffering, gentleness, goodness, faith,
Meekness, temperance: against such there
is no law. Galatians 5:22-23

When we are not living in the Spirit, the only other thing we can be doing is living in the flesh. There isn't any middle ground. Putting on Christ daily is the only way to keep from being bogged down with sin.

And they that are Christ's have crucified the flesh
with the affections and lusts. If we live in the
Spirit, let us also walk in the Spirit. Galatians 5:24-25

I trust that I can have my pantry full of the wonderful Fruit of the Spirit. I know it isn't easy. We have to put some energy into it. Those green beans will not string themselves or hop into the jars by themselves. Preserving takes a little work, and so does living in the Spirit and allowing Christ to have full reign.

Just like putting up home canned goods, it takes a little heat, a little pressure, and above all a little sterilizing of the jars and equipment to get started.

We can only live in the Spirit when we have all unconfessed sin taken care. That's like sterilizing and making things ready to put up that good fruit into the canning jars. Confessed sin is what we need to be able to have that fruit properly stored and displayed in our lives.

I hope I can live that way. When people open my pantry cupboard as it were, I'd like them to find all those jars of things that only living in the Spirit can produce lined up on the shelves.

So, what are you making provision for?

2

ON TARGET

*My glory was fresh in me, and my bow
was renewed in my hand. Job 29:20*

Arrows seem to be really popular in graphics and images today. We see them on chalkboard art and in home decor and just about everywhere. *The Hunger Games* movies have probably made arrows a little more popular too.

Let's take a look at Job 29:20, where Job says, "...my bow was renewed in my hand." What does a bow do? It shoots arrows of course, and you have to have strength to shoot an arrow. Sure, shooting arrows requires accuracy and good aim, but ultimately it requires strength to pull back on the bow.

Living the Christian life requires strength too. We cannot do it on our own. We have to depend upon the Lord in order to draw strength. We need that fellowship with Him. We have to rely on the Lord to build us up and to help us wield our arrows

9

through life.

So how do we keep that strength renewed in our hands? I think the parts of an arrow can help us. There are four parts.

(1) **Fletching**

The fletching is that feathery part of an arrow. It is used to provide a little force to stabilize the arrow as it flies through the air.

What are we using for our "fletching"? What stabilizes us as Christians?   It has got to be the Word of God. Nothing else can ground us more and help us as we fly through life.

> *For the word of God is quick, and powerful, and*
> *sharper than any twoedged sword, piercing even*
> *to the dividing asunder of soul and spirit, and of the*
> *joints and marrow, and is a discerner of the thoughts*
> *and intents of the heart. Hebrews 4:12*

(2) **Arrowhead**

The next part is the arrowhead. It is the point at the end of an arrow. The type of arrowhead an arrow has attached depends on the purpose for which it is used.

What is our purpose as Christians? It should be to live for Christ and bring others to Him. We are ambassadors for Christ. Let's look at that passage in 2 Corinthians 5. It talks about this.

>And that he died for all, that they which live
>should not henceforth live unto themselves,
>but unto him which died for them, and
>rose again. *2 Corinthians 5:15*

>Now then we are ambassadors for Christ, as
>though God did beseech you by us: we pray
>you in Christ' stead, be ye reconciled
>to God. *2 Corinthians 5:20*

(3) **Nock**

The nock is the back end of the arrow. It is the little cut-out spot that you insert into the string before you shoot the arrow. It holds the arrow in place while you take your aim and draw the bow.

What keeps us in place? I think our prayer life can do that. Spending time in prayer helps us build our relationship to Christ and helps us increase our faith.

I find, especially as I get older, that prayer steadies me. I don't know how I would cope with life without being able to go to the Lord in prayer.

> *Let us therefore come boldly unto the throne of grace, that we may obtain mercy, and find grace to help in time of need. Hebrews 4:16*

(4) **Shaft**

The shaft of an arrow is that long part. It is the part to which the other elements are attached.

Salvation is our shaft. Salvation is what we build upon as a Christian. We have to have that in place first.

Accepting Christ is key before we can build a relationship with Him and begin serving Him. We have to have our Salvation settled.

> *But as many as received him, to them gave he power to become the sons of God, even to them that believe on this name: John 1:12*

Final Thoughts

I know I am constantly in need of having my bow "renewed" as I go about my daily life. I have to rely on God's strength in order to function. I find myself down, weary, and just about to give up when I don't depend on the strength of the Lord.

I want to be able to go through life with my aim in the right direction, and I can only do that when I fellowship and walk closely to the Lord.

Maybe you aren't attached to the shaft. You haven't accepted Christ for your Salvation. I urge you to make that decision. Only through Christ can your life take on direction and meaning.

I think sometimes it is good to stop and reflect what we are living for. Are we grounded in the Word so that we shoot through life with force? What type of arrow point do we have? Are we dull and blunt? What kind of an impact do we make? Are we serving our purpose? Are we staying on target in our Christian life?

I can remember going to camp when I was a kid and learning a little bit about archery. I remember one of the things was to work on our stance. How you stand when shooting an arrow is important. That reminds me of the passage in Ephesians 6 about our Christian armor. It is all about how we stand.

> *Wherefore take unto you the whole armour of God,*
> *that ye may be able to withstand in the evil day,*
> *and having done all, to stand. Ephesians 6:13*

If you read on through that passage it describes several things that all revolve on how we should stand as Christians.

It all boils down to relying on Christ to stabilize us and keep us on target.

Look what it says in Isaiah 40:31.

> *But they that wait upon the LORD shall renew*
> *their strength; they shall mount up with wings*
> *as eagles; they shall run, and not be weary;*
> *and they shall walk, and not faint.*

So, is your bow being renewed in your hand?

3
JUST BECAUSE

Withhold not good from them to whom it is due, when
it is in the power of thine hand to do it. Proverbs 3:27

One of the best ways to encourage and motivate others involves being a blessing to them. I was raised with a philosophy that we make "just because" moments happen for other people.

My dad was real good about doing things like that. Out of the blue he'd drop someone off a bag of green beans or tomatoes from the garden. When he would fish, sometimes he'd show up on someone's doorstep with a mess of fish all scaled, cleaned, and ready to fry up in a pan or put in the freezer.

I know I've been the recipient of many wonderful *just because* moments and they were abundant blessings given to me straight from the Lord by way of a good friend or sometimes from people I didn't even know very well. It's amazing how the Lord knows just when we need a *just because* moment to lift our spirits and motivate us in some way.

When I went into the hospital for diverticulitis several years ago, a lady from our church had given me a card with verses and poems written on some pages of notepaper she had enclosed. At the time I just glanced at them because I wasn't feeling well.

A couple of weeks after I was home and recovering, I went back and actually read through the cards I'd received while in the hospital. This lady had taken the time to hand write out several poems and verses.

When I read through them, it was just what I needed at that very moment, and I appreciated that she took the time to sit and hand write all of that out for me. It was a wonderful *just because* moment for me to receive the blessing of encouragement that those shared words gave.

We ought to get hold of making *just because* moments happen for other people. If we can be a blessing to others, we need to be one.

Withhold not good from them to whom
it is due, when it is in the power of thine
hand to do it. Proverbs 3:27

Being a blessing doesn't even necessarily have to cost anything. Just spending time with someone can be a wonderful *just because* moment. Little things can mean so much to people. Praying for someone and then letting him or her know you did can just bless someone's heart.

Sometimes just an encouraging word or even a "hello" and a listening ear is all it takes to bless someone in a significant way. We don't always know what's happening internally in someone's life, and when we put out the effort to be a blessing and they are at that point where they really need some encouragement, it can make a big difference in their lives.

A man hath joy by the answer of his
mouth: and a word spoken in due
season, how good is it! Proverbs 15:23

I think sometimes we get so busy going about just doing that we forget the importance of doing for others. We forget the importance that people are what really count in this life. Being a blessing to other people is such a wonderful way to show the love of God flowing through us.

Look not every man on his own things, but every man also on the things of others. Let this mind be in you, which was also in Christ Jesus: Philippians 2:4-5

Be sure to read through Philippians 2:1-5.

<u>Final Thoughts</u>

I know it is easy to get so caught up in our own lives that we forget those around us need encouragement. I hope I can get a handle on this. I hope the Lord will see fit to use me to make *just because* moments happen for others.

I'd like to strive to really be aware of other people's feelings and need for that lift of encouragement that we all desire from time to time. I know I'm in need of that encouragement quite often.

So, when's the last time you made a *just because* moment happen for someone?

4
HOW BRIGHT IS YOUR LIGHT?

Let your light so shine before men, that they
may see your good works, and glorify your
Father which is in heaven. Matthew 5:16

As Christians, we know we are to shine as beacons of light in this sinful world, but how bright do we shine?

Our verse says, "Let your light so shine before men...", but do we really look any different to our co-workers and neighbors than anyone else they come in contact with?

Is our speech different? Is our attitude different? When things go wrong in our lives do others see that we have something or Someone to lean on? Do people see that we as Christians have something they don't have?

Many of us learned the little song when we were small about not hiding our light under a bushel, but as adults that's exactly what we do sometimes. We get so caught up in living in this world that we forget that we are not *of* this world. We have something better in Christ, but our sinful nature rears its ugly head and we forget we are children of the King.

We need to realize that this world is dark with sin and people need us as Christians to shine. As we look around at the school shootings, drugs, crime, and the diluting of the family, we are reminded of how there are hurting people all around.

People need the Lord and they need hope. We as children of God can give that to them if we just live as a shining example of Christ. We can't keep Christ to ourselves. We have to flood the world with His Light!

What kind of light are you?

Are you a smokey lamp with a cloudy globe?

When a lamp's globe is clouded up it doesn't shine to its fullest potential. Maybe the blackness of unconfessed sin has crept in and started smoking up your life.

It just takes a little smoke to cloud up a lamp

globe.

The same is true with our lives. It just takes a little sin to make our light dull. We are always going to be prone to sin because it's our nature, but we have to work on it one day at a time.

We have to confess our sin to Christ. Having unconfessed sin breaks our fellowship with Christ and causes our lives not to shine our brightest for Him.

> *If we confess our sins, he is faithful and just to forgive us our sins, and to cleanse us from all unrighteousness. 1 John 1:9*

Are you a dim and slow burning candle?

As a candle burns out it gets dim and burns slow. Are you this type of light? Remember when you first received Christ? The Christian life was exciting and new! Are you getting slow about having a devotional life? Is your prayer life getting dim?

It's easy to become complacent in our Christian life, but when we do, our light for Christ begins to dim and others can't see Him in us. Take a step back, get things into perspective, and remember what Christ did for you.

> *But God commendeth his love toward*
> *us, in that, while we were yet sinners,*
> *Christ died for us. Romans 5:8*

Are you a flickering and hazy light bulb?

Just before a light bulb blows out, it flickers. It shines bright then dull and hazy, then bright and then dull again. Are you that type of light for Christ? Do you serve Him wholeheartedly, then slack off?

Maybe you get discouraged about something and you start flickering. Then you get fired up again and begin really serving the Lord only to be bogged down again.

You may find yourself not attending church, not reading your Bible, slacking off in your prayer life and fellowship with the Lord.

The Christian life wasn't designed to be lived on and off again. It has to be a daily continual thing.

Look what it says in Luke 9:23. It says, "daily".

And he said to them all, If any man
will come after me, let him deny
himself, and take up his cross
daily, and follow me. Luke 9:23

Are you a bright and shining beacon?

When you think of a beacon you usually think of a light that is a bright and shining guide. That is the type of light that we should all desire to be. Being constantly in fellowship with Christ and sensitive to His leading will keep our lives as beacons to a lost and dying world.

To do this, we have to work at it. Souls depend on us. In order to shine brightly for Christ, we have to be a B-E-A-C-O-N.

(B) Battle

(E) Endure

(A) Abstain

(C) Consecrate

(O) Obey

(N) Nurture

Battle (Remember what you are battling against.)

Be sober, be vigilant; because your adversary
the devil, as a roaring lion, walketh about,
seeking whom he may devour: 1 Peter 5:8

Endure (Keep pressing on.)

Brethren, I count not myself to have apprehended:
but this one thing I do, forgetting those things which
are behind, and reaching forth unto those things which
are before, I press toward the mark for the prize of the
high calling of God in Christ Jesus. Philippians. 3:13-14

Abstain (Don't get caught up in the world.)

Abstain from all appearance
of evil. 1 Thessalonians 5:22

Consecrate (Live a holy life.)

I beseech you therefore, brethren, by the mercies
of God, that ye present your bodies a living
sacrifice, holy, acceptable unto God, which is
your reasonable service. Romans 12:1

Obey (Be obedient to Christ.)

*... bringing into captivity every thought to the
obedience of Christ; 2 Corinthians 10:5*

Nurture (Stay in the Word.)

*Study to show thyself approved unto God, a
workman that needeth not to be ashamed, rightly
dividing the word of truth. 2 Timothy 2:15*

<u>Final Thoughts</u>

When we go back to that first verse we started
with, Matthew 5:16, we see the importance of our
light shining.

*Let your light so shine before men, that they
may see your good works, and glorify your
Father which is in heaven. Matthew 5:16*

The world needs to see our good works, and
ultimately it is all about glorifying God.

So, how bright is your light?

5
SMALL LITTLE TRIFLES

He that is faithful in that which is least is
faithful also in much: and he that is unjust
in the least is unjust also in much. Luke 16:10

Today we are going to talk about the small things in life. Things we consider trifles. Little things we say. Little things we do. When you think about it, so many small things in life kind of connect with the bigger things. I think about the things we do that are little and simple but can accomplish so much.

There is the smile on our face. When you wear a smile you become approachable and that can sometimes make all the difference in the world to another person.

What about the tiny things we say? In James 3 it talks about the tongue being a "little member", but there is so much good or so much damage our tongues can cause.

David killed Goliath with just one smooth stone. (1 Samuel 17). Jesus fed the multitude with the loaves of bread and the "few small fishes" (Mark 8). And look how we are supposed to notice the tiny ant and learn great wisdom from it.

Go to the ant, thou sluggard; consider her ways, and be wise: Which having no guide, overseer, or ruler, Provideth her meat in the summer, and gathereth her food in the harvest. Proverbs 6:6-8

When we read through Luke 16 about the unjust steward, we see how when we are faithful in the little things, we will be faithful in the big things.

He that is faithful in that which is least is faithful also in much: and he that is unjust in the least is unjust also in much. Luke 16:10

Everything we do in life is not always fun or exciting. Sometimes those small things are just plain tedious but need to be done. You might have at the moment, or might have had, one of those "dirty jobs" Mike Rowe talks about. Maybe you are in an aspect of ministry that is not what anyone would characterize as glamorous, but God needs someone in that role.

I think about just the common ordinary things we use in our daily lives that are small things but they have big jobs. Look at the paperclip or staple. They keep us organized and from losing important papers. What about those buttons and fasteners? They have that big job of keeping us dressed. What about a tiny seed? It can grow great things.

Have you ever heard that expression, "It's all in the details"? The details are those little things that combined altogether make up the big things.

When it comes to being faithful there are some things we can't overlook.

Being Faithful in Your Prayer Life

Now I consider prayer a big thing, but when it comes down to it, you don't have to do anything large or grand to engage in it. You just have to use your mouth or even just talk to God silently. I'm not going to list all the fantastic, big, large, and overwhelming things that prayer can do. I'm sure you already know that.

Being Faithful in Your Worship

Worship is powerful but can be done anywhere, planned, or on the spur of the moment. You don't even have to be inside of a church building to be faithful in worship.

Being Faithful in the Word

We can all get into the Word of God. In the age we live in, the Bible is accessible to just about everyone. You can even read it on your computer or for that matter get an app of it for your phone. Just a little time each day in God's Word can impact your life in a big and powerful way.

Being Faithful to Give Thanks

Thanking God for His blessings should be a little habit that we all have as Christians. Start counting your blessings and your thankful heart will grow by leaps and bounds. One thing that may help is to make a daily blessing list.

Being Faithful in Your Giving

There is monetary giving to think about, and God doesn't ask for much, just tithes and offerings. It's really so little, especially when we consider all of the other ways we spend our money.

Giving your time is important too. A few hours of good deeds can accomplish much.

Being Faithful in Spreading the Gospel

All we have to do to spread the Gospel is to just plant one little seed at a time. It might be literally telling someone else about Christ. It might be by being an example of a Spirit-led Christian in your daily life. Maybe it is handing out Gospel tracts and witnessing door to door.

Look how many we all could lead to Christ if we just started witnessing a little at a time.

Final Thoughts

I am sure there are many other areas in our lives in which we need to be faithful as Christians. We just need to examine our own hearts to see what we need to work on.

I love reading through Hebrews 11, and I find myself reading through it more and more lately. The faith of those mentioned there always inspires me and encourages me in my own faith. I always feel so empowered after reading through that chapter about all of those faith heroes.

Have you ever noticed those last several verses of Hebrews 11? These people's lives were not easy, but they were faithful. Some of us think we have it bad. Look what these people went through for their faith.

> *...and others were tortured, not accepting*
> *deliverance; that they might obtain a better*
> *resurrection: And others had trial of cruel*
> *mockings and scourgings, yea, moreover of*
> *bonds an imprisonment: They were stoned,*
> *they were sawn asunder, were tempted, were*
> *slain with the sword: they wandered about*
> *in sheepskins and goatskins; being destitute,*
> *afflicted, tormented; (Of whom the world*
> *was not worthy:) they wandered in deserts,*
> *and in mountains, and in dens*
> *and caves of the earth. Hebrews 11:35-38*

In verses 33 and 34, we see what big and powerful things their faith did.

Who through faith subdued kingdoms, wrought righteousness, obtained promises, stopped the mouths of lions, Quenched the violence of fire, escaped the edge of the sword, out of weakness were made the strong, waxed valiant in fight, turned to flight the armies of aliens. Hebrews 11:33-34

I want so much for my own faith to grow like that. I'm sure these people were faithful in the little things. Look at what they accomplished through their faith in God.

We don't get to see the whole picture of how little things add up in our lives. We may think something is just a trifle of a thing, but God might have something marvelous worked out down the road that we just can't see or may never see.

So, are you faithful in the little things?

6
WINDOW VIEWS

And we know that all things work together for
good to them that love God, to them who are the
called according to his purpose. Romans 8:28

As we go through life, we can't always know what we are going to wake up to outside our window, but we will each have some type of view. That, you can count on! Some views are stunning and beautiful. Other times they are ugly and not very pleasant.

Sometimes there are clouds and rain or there is snow piling up. Other times there are things blocking our view and we can't see what's out there or see very far. Many things that come into our lives are permanent, but others seem to fade out of view.

Let's peek through some windows and see some different views throughout Scripture.

The Window of Purpose

Noah's View - Genesis 8

Look at the window in the ark. God had Noah

build the ark and put that window right there because later on that window was going to have a purpose. Remember how Noah first sent out a raven through the window? Then he sent the dove.

And it came to pass at the end of forty days, that Noah opened the window of the ark which he had made: And he sent forth a raven, which went forth to and fro, until the waters were dried up from off the earth. Also he sent forth a dove from him, to see if the waters were abated from off the face of the ground; But the dove found no rest for the sole of her foot, and she returned unto him into the ark, for the waters were on the face of the whole earth: then he put forth his hand, and took her, and pulled her in unto him into the ark. Genesis 8:6-9

Next Noah sent the dove out the window and it came back with an olive branch, so Noah knew that the waters had receded from the flood. The next time Noah sent out the dove, it didn't come back. There was a clear purpose for that window.

Sometimes in our lives we get a view from our window and we look out, we see what's going on, and we know what the purpose is. Other times we may not get that luxury. We don't always understand why God sends things into our lives. They are right there in our view, but we just can't see the purpose.

God had a complete design for the ark. He told Noah exactly how to build it even down to where he placed that window. God always knows the exact purpose. We just get frustrated because we are not in on the design end of things.

The Window of Truth
Abimelech's View - Genesis 26

There are going to be times when we look out our view and see truth. Sometimes the truth is hard to swallow, especially if it is something about a loved one, or you learn facts about something that is difficult for you to believe.

Remember how Isaac and Rebekah pretended to be brother and sister? Isaac lied because he was afraid he would be killed because Rebekah was so beautiful. When Abimelech looked out his window, the truth was easy to spot with Isaac and Rebekah.

Other times it might be hard to see at first, but truth usually has a way of coming to the surface.

And it came to pass, when he had been there a long time, that Abimelech king of the Philistines looked out at a window, and saw, and, behold, Isaac was sporting with Rebekah his wife. And Abimelech called Isaac, and said, Behold, of a surety she is thy wife: and how saidst thou, She is my sister? And Isaac said unto him, Because I said, Lest I die for her. Genesis 26:8-9

Sometimes truths that we see are wonderful. We get joy from them. Other times some ugly truths come into the view of our lives. It might be something like a sickness. Maybe you are even a victim of an affair that you have to deal with. Perhaps it might be the truth of how someone you love has chosen to live their life apart from Christ.

I have seen preachers who I thought were phenomenal Christians get away from Christ, and I hated seeing it. I just felt like I was crushed when I looked out and realized someone I had looked up to had fallen so completely away from Christ.

When truth comes into our view, it can hurt. We want to close the curtains, pull down the blinds, or even board up the windows so we can't see that view, but it's still there.

Only the Lord can help us deal with those ugly views of truth when they lurk outside our window. We have to give it over to Him if we want to see past that view and not let it hinder us.

The Window of Silence

Rahab's View - Joshua 2

There are times when we see things outside our window that we are going to have to keep to ourselves. We won't be able to share that view. We are going to have to keep silent about it.

Are you familiar with the story of how Rahab helped the spies in Joshua chapter 2? Joshua had sent out two men to spy out the country of Jericho. Unfortunately the King of Jericho found out about them, but a woman named Rahab hid the spies.

I love this story because it shows that God can use anyone and any type of person. Rahab was a harlot but still God used her. And no matter what she was, she still recognized who God was. In Joshua 2:9-10, Rahab is talking to the spies and telling them how they had heard of all the things that God had done, and in verse 11, she tells them,

And as soon as we had heard these things, our hearts did melt, neither did there remain any more courage in any man, because of you: for the LORD your God, he is God in heaven above, and in earth beneath. Joshua 2:11

The story goes on. Rahab wanted them to remember her and her family with kindness when Joshua's men ended up taking over the city. She then helped the spies through a window to escape.

And the men answered her, Our life for yours, if ye utter not this our business. And it shall be, when the LORD hath given us the land, that we will deal kindly and truly with thee. Then she let them down by a cord through the window: for her house was upon the town wall, and she dwelt upon the wall. Joshua 2:14-15

There are going to be times when someone

confides in you or you learn something that you know you need to keep to yourself. You know you shouldn't *utter* a word. You are going to have to discipline yourself to keep things to yourself.

That something might be right there in your view, but you know that it is a view you are not at liberty to share. Sometimes you are not going to be able to take anyone else to the window with you.

I know standing at the window alone and having to keep something to yourself can sometimes be hard, but the only one you can talk to about it is the Lord. Talk to Him about whatever it is you can't talk to another human about.

The Window of Unexpectedness

Eutychus' View - Acts 20:7-12

Every time I read through Acts 20 or hear someone preach on it, I have to chuckle. Here we see Paul preaching with a man present named Eutychus. Now this man had found a seat to listen to the sermon in a window of the upper chamber and had fallen asleep.

I don't really blame this man for falling asleep, because it does say in verse 7 of that chapter that Paul preached from the time they broke bread until about midnight. In verse 9 it says, "Paul was long preaching". Friends, it wasn't a short sermon!

So here they were, Paul preaching away, and Eutychus sleeping away, when all of a sudden the man fell from the window.

And there sat in a window a certain young man named Eutychus, being fallen into a deep sleep: and as Paul was long preaching, he sunk down with sleep, and fell down from the third loft, and was taken up dead. And Paul went down, and fell on him, and embracing him said, Trouble not yourselves; for his life is in him. Acts 20:9-10

Now Paul said that the man wasn't dead, but wouldn't that be such a jolt? Have you had "views" like that where life is going along smoothly and all of a sudden you are falling out the window?

Life seems to be crashing down all around you? Like the man in Acts, you might not end up dead, but you land with such a thud that you feel like you've lost your life.

When things that are unexpected come into our views, it shocks us sometimes. We are so startled that we don't know what to do. At times like that I don't think there's anything to do but go to the Lord.

Tell Him how shaken up you are. Let Him comfort you and help you work through it.

The Window of Threat

Daniel's View - Daniel 6

Prayer played a big part in Daniel's life. I'm sure you remember the story. There were men out to get Daniel so they had the king sign a decree that no one was to pray or ask anything of any man or god for thirty days.

The king signed it into law, but Daniel still prayed to God as he always had. Not only that, but he didn't do it hidden away. Daniel prayed with his windows open.

Now when Daniel knew that the writing was signed,
he went into his house; and his windows being open in

his chamber toward Jerusalem, he kneeled upon his knees three times a day, and prayed, and gave thanks before his God, as he did aforetime. Then these men assembled, and found Daniel praying and making supplication before his God. Daniel 6:10-11

We know that everything turned out okay for Daniel. He was thrown in the lion's den, but God protected him. On top of that, those evil men and their families were all thrown in with the lions and they didn't have the Lord to protect them.

Of course I think when Daniel was praying that he probably knew those men were lurking outside of his window. They were a threat waiting to pounce, but Daniel kept doing what he knew was right. He didn't let that view derail Him from his prayer life.

I think that sometimes we get things that come into our lives and they threaten to destroy us and it hurts our prayer life.

We get side-tracked and don't spend that time with the Lord that we know we need. We can't let those views that threaten us get in the way of our fellowship with Christ.

The view in a *window of threat* can be a scary place to be.

The Window of Protection

Paul's View - 2 Corinthians 11

I love it when I go to my window and see the Lord's hand of protection. In 2 Corinthians, Paul talks about a time when the Lord protected him. There was a garrison of men after him, but God used a basket and a window to protect Paul.

> *In Damascus the governor under Aretas the king*
> *kept the city of the Damascenes with a garrison,*
> *desirous to apprehend me: And through a window*
> *in a basket was I let down by the wall, and*
> *escaped his hands. 2 Corinthians 11:32-33*

There are so many "baskets" I know of that the Lord has used to deliver me. Sometimes I think, well, how did I live through that? I know it was only by the Lord's protecting arm around me.

Sometimes all the pieces aren't in view. I may not actually see how the Lord did it, but I can see the result and I love that view of protection.

We see all through the Bible so many examples of God's protection.

Final Thoughts

Some of the views we get in life are great views. They are beautiful and make us want to keep running with excitement to the window in the mornings to pull open the shades to see what's waiting for us.

Other times there are some views that really can make us almost frozen so that we can't move on. They make us feel so afraid that we can't see past to the beautiful view of all the blessings in our lives.

There may be things that we no longer appreciate because we are dwelling on that view so much that we forget about some of the important things we are already blessed with. We sometimes even forget about the Lord, and it is only Christ that can help us with our *views*.

The Lord may have some beautiful things out there for us to look at and enjoy, but we are so full of hurt or fear that we don't see the beauty that's right there in front of us.

I think about that old poem, *The Weaving*, by Grant Colfax Tullar. It talks about how our lives are like a weaving where we may only see the underside but the Lord sees the upper side. Only the Lord knows why each color of thread is used and why we need certain things in our lives. God sees how it all is working together.

I know as Christians we quote that verse in Romans 8:28 a lot, but I think sometimes that "all" in the verse makes us cringe. "All" things that come into our lives are sometimes not the perfect view that we want to look out and see.

> *And we know that all things work together for*
> *good to them that love God, to them who are the*
> *called according to his purpose. Romans 8:28*

I don't want to miss those things outside my window, like the pretty cherry trees that are full of blossoms, the birds and butterflies floating about, the flowers that are in full bloom, the green of the grass, and the beauty of the sunset. I hope you don't want to miss any of those breath-taking views either.

There may be some bad things that come into our lives, but let's not miss the good things by dwelling on the unpleasant views. Let's enjoy those blessings the Lord gives and allow Christ to be with us when we look out our windows of life.

So, what's in your view?

7

WATCH OUT FOR THE WILES!

*Put on the whole armour of God, that ye may be able
to stand against the wiles of the devil. Ephesians 6:11*

There are just so many things that can ensnare us as Christians. The devil makes sure of that. Ephesians 6:11, talks about the "wiles of the devil".

Those *wiles* are those tricky, sly, and deceitful things that draw us away from Christ. The devil is very good at throwing his *wiles* our way.

It seems we always have to be on our toes. We can't just sit back and live in a relaxed mode because we'll get "wiled" if we do. The devil is out there seeking us like a roaring lion as it says in 1 Peter 5:8.

What will the W-I-L-E-S do to us?

(W) Woo us into ungodly thinking.

We don't use that word *woo* much anymore, but that's exactly what the devil does to us. It doesn't happen all at once. He slowly gets our affection by wooing us with his subtle means. Maybe by television, internet ads, magazines, ungodly advice, and worldly philosophy in general.

If we don't watch it, pretty soon we are thinking just like the world thinks.

(I) Introduce us to things not of Christ.

Introducing revolves around getting acquainted with something or someone. The devil slyly introduces us to worldly things just one glance at a time. We may not even react to it at first. We get acquainted with it little by little and pretty soon we begin to know that worldly thing more intimately.

I know we all think we know right from wrong, but sometimes the devil can blur our decision making process, and pretty soon we find we're involved in things that are not of Christ.

(L) Lure us into ungodly deeds.

When I think of the word *lure*, I think about how much my dad used to love to fish so much and he'd have all those lures that he would use. Those are artificial bait if you're not familiar with a fishing lure.

I can remember how some of them were so pretty with all kinds of colors and flair. My dad was always so proud of his lures and anything in his tackle boxes. He would take them out and say, "Now I use this one for" such and such kind of fish. And he'd use another one for another kind of fish and so on. I can remember him explaining what type of lure that each type of fish was attracted to.

That is what the devil uses to catch us too. He uses artificial bait. Those are those things that are appealing but that have no real value to them. And that devil knows which one to put on his hook just tailor made for each of us too.

He knows exactly what will attract us. Pretty soon we see all those pretty colors and feathers and we're lured away and involved in ungodly deeds.

(E) Exclude us from fellowship with Christ.

Most people don't like to be excluded from things. *Excluding* means we are prevented from taking part or participating. Nobody likes to be on the outside. We all have this need to be part of what's going on. We want the choice of whether to be a part of something. We don't like other people making that choice for us.

When we are enticed by those wiles of the devil, we end up far away from Christ and that means a broken relationship with Him. The thing is, we are the one that made that choice. We chose to be *excluded*.

We have got to confess the sin in our lives or we can't have that fellowship with our Lord that we need. Sin and Christ don't mix. Christ is holy. Being excluded from fellowship with the Lord is a scary place to be.

(S)   Snare us into worldly living.

A *snare* is used to trap or entangle. When we don't watch out for those wiles of the devil, we sure can get entangled. We can get entangled right into ungodly living if we aren't careful.

Pretty soon it is not just an isolated ungodly

thought or an isolated ungodly deed. It becomes a whole ungodly lifestyle we're leading. We can't serve two masters. We're either going to live for Christ or live for the world.

Final Thoughts

When we aren't watching out for those *wiles* of the devil we can be so easily caught up into them. I know I need to be a little more careful and keep on my toes. As Christians, we all do.

We've got to keep putting on that "whole armor" that's mentioned in the rest of Ephesians chapter 6.

So, are you watching out for the *wiles*?

8

SET SAIL FOR SERVING

We then that are strong ought to bear
the infirmities of the weak, and not to
please ourselves. Romans 15:1

When we hear about Christian stewardship, we usually hear mainly about the use of our money, time, and talents. I'd like to focus on the idea of just being a steward like on a ship. What do they do? Basically stewards are there to serve others.

Isn't that so important in the Christian life? It seems like the money, time, and talents just fall into place when we are busy serving others.

I went and checked online at some of the various cruise lines to see what their qualifications were for hiring stewards. Here are some things I found that were the same across the board. You'll notice they are traits that as Christians we should have as well.

Must be friendly and get along with people.

That's a good place to start when you are working

on improving your Christian life. Work on just being friendly. How are we ever going to share Christ if we are not friendly to those people that God has placed in our path?

Friendliness can start with just simple things like maybe just sharing a smile or going out of your way to say hello. It can lead on up to other things. Isn't that the example Christ left for us when He washed the dirt from off the disciples' feet in John 13?

You'll notice the requirement is not just being friendly, but getting along with people. As Christians that shouldn't be too hard for us, but sometimes it is. It's not just the idea of getting along with people of the world that we come in contact with, but we have to get along with other Christians as well.

If there be therefore any consolation in Christ, if any comfort of love, if any fellowship of the Spirit, if any bowels and mercies, Fulfill ye my joy, that ye be likeminded, having the same love, being of one accord, of one mind. Let nothing be done through strife or vainglory; but in lowliness of mind let each esteem other better than themselves. Look not every man on his own things, but every man also on the things of others. Let this mind be in you, which was also in Christ Jesus: Philippians 2:1-5

Must be in contact with people all the time.

Oh no! We can't go hide from people if we are going to do the job of a steward. Isn't that what the Great Commission is all about? Reaching people?

We have to be in contact with people in order to share our faith and reach them for Christ. We can't keep the wonderful news of Christ to ourselves. It was meant to share.

And he said unto them, Go ye into all the world, and preach the gospel to every creature. Mark 16:15

Must be able to take criticism.

If as stewards we are going to be dealing with a lot of people, criticism is just naturally going to come along in some form or another. In order to serve others as a steward should, we are sometimes going to have to bite our tongues. We have to stop and remember Who we are ultimately serving.

I'm not talking about letting people run over us, but there are ways that we should conduct ourselves as Christians. The manner in which we talk, react, and behave when it comes to dealing with people is important. Look at Proverbs 15:1.

A soft answer turneth away wrath:
but grievous words stir up anger.

If we are going to be stewards for Christ, a big part of our job description is getting our tongues and actions under control.

Must be able to work long hours.

Being a Christian steward isn't always going to be easy. There are going to be times when we are called upon to serve someone else when it may not be convenient for us. Someone may need you to give them a ride to church or the grocery store. It may be your turn in the church nursery. Someone may be sick and you may be the next one on the list to bring the chicken soup.

We may not always feel like serving, but we must keep on going. We are serving Christ by serving others.

And let us not be weary in well doing: for in due season we shall reap, if we faint not. As we have therefore opportunity, let us do good unto all men, especially unto them who are of the household of faith. Galatians 6:9-10

Must be able to serve the wants and needs of others.

We have become a "me" society, so when it comes to serving the needs of others it may seem a little foreign to us. It shouldn't be though.

As Christians, it should be a natural part of us to want to serve others. It's the whole crux of what Christ taught us to be. He didn't even live to please Himself.

We then that are strong ought to bear the infirmities of the weak, and not to please ourselves. Let every one of us please his neighbour for his good to edification. For even Christ pleased not himself... Romans 15:1-3

Final Thoughts

A steward that works on a ship knows that the things left in his charge are not his, but he takes care of those things just as though they belong to him.

Christ gives us our time, wealth, and health. What we do with those things is important because we don't own them. They are given to us to use here on this earth. A big part of how we use those things is in regard to serving others.

Serving others can be rewarding in so many ways. It may not always be easy, but it is part of the lifestyle we should embrace as Christians. We have to keep in mind our eternal rewards.

Remember what Christ taught us in Matthew 25? Serving others is how we ultimately serve Christ.

For I was an hungred, and ye gave me meat: I was thirsty, and ye gave me drink: I was a stranger, and ye took me in: Naked, and ye clothed me: I was sick, and ye visited me: I was in prison, and ye came unto me.
Then shall the righteous answer him, saying, Lord, when saw we thee an hungred, and fed thee? or thirsty, and gave thee drink? When saw we thee a stranger, and took thee in? or naked, and clothed thee? Or when saw

we thee sick, or in prison, and came unto thee? And the King shall answer and say unto them, Verily I say unto you, Inasmuch as ye have done it unto one of the least of these my brethren, ye have done it unto me. Matthew 25:35-40

So, do you have the qualities of a good steward?

9

MAKING FUDGE

And be ye kind one to another, tenderhearted,
forgiving one another, even as God for Christ's
sake hath forgiven you. Ephesians 4:32

Election years bring out the numbers. Don't they? We all know what *fudging the numbers* means, especially when someone begins running for office. Whether it is job numbers or whatever. You can always spin something to make it sound better.

And what about those poll numbers? I always think they are nothing more than arranged and rearranged numbers. We are never given all the details of how those polls are taken. Most of them miss the mass population so they are really mostly worthless. At least to me.

I fear that sometimes we get like that in our Christian lives. We want to "fudge" the numbers. We want to make ourselves sound a little better at something than we really are. Maybe not necessarily to other people, but sometimes we try to rationalize things in our own heads.

Salvation

Some people rationalize their Salvation. They rely on what their parents believed or what they grew up with to get them to heaven, but when it comes down to it, Salvation is a choice we must all make. We each have to make a personal decision to accept Christ.

Salvation is one thing we do not want to rationalize on because the consequence of spending eternity away from Christ is severe. If you just *think* you are a Christian, maybe it is time to really get that settled. It is better to know-so than think-so.

Witnessing

Have you ever fudged your idea of the amount you witness for Christ? I know we are all to have that Christian living which reflects Christ, but face it, we have to tell other people about Christ too.

Are you counting up the smiles you give and good deeds you do for others as your total witness? I know we all have heard that quote, "You may be the only Bible someone ever reads", but really we have to be an *open* Bible not a *closed* book. We have to share Christ with others in some way or other.

Or maybe because you attend a weekly visitation program and do a little visiting and witnessing, you think you have done your part and mark that column filled, but you forget about the whole Christian living thing the rest of the week.

I know witnessing is hard and I struggle with it, but we are supposed to be spreading the Gospel. It is part of being a Christian.

Obedience

Are you really an obedient Christian? I know I'm not always obedient, but I think we all kind of tell ourselves that we are more obedient than we really are.

Are we really doing what Christ wants us to on a daily basis? Are we as sensitive to the Holy Spirit as we should be?

The Lord may not ask us to go to Nineveh like He

did Jonah, or even call us to the mission field, but are we really obedient in the little things as well as the big things like we should be? Do we miss opportunities to share Christ because we aren't obedient? Do we follow all the teachings of Christ or just choose what we want to obey?

Prayer

As Christians, we all know prayer is part of our daily lives, and if I asked any church ladies group if prayer was important, I'd probably get an emphatic *yes* answer. But how important is it to us really? Do we pray enough? Do we pray like we should? Do we pray for others when we know we should? Do we ask for the things in prayer that we should? Do we thank the Lord in prayer for things as we should?

We all know the example Christ set for us in Matthew 6 for prayer, but do we really follow it? Or are we just hurrying about through our prayer life? Maybe getting in a little prayer here and there, but not really giving it as much attention and thought as we do preparing dinner or working on our hobbies.

We are supposed to "pray without ceasing" (1 Thessalonians 5:17), which doesn't mean we are to constantly have our eyes closed and heads bowed, but have a prayerful attitude and always be in constant communion with the Lord.

I love what Charles Spurgeon says about this passage. "If I am to pray without ceasing, then every second must be suitable for prayer, and there is not one unholy moment in the hour, nor one unaccepted hour in the day, nor one unhallowed day in the year."

Bible Reading

The priority of our Bible reading is another place I think we as Christians try to *fudge*. We put it far up on our list of things to do as a Christian, but do we really keep it a priority? This is one I struggle with.

I try to make sure I keep a time set during the day to read through my Bible, but I have to make myself keep on top of it or that Bible time slips away.

Sometimes I find it is the end of another day without spending time in the Word.

Years ago I used to follow devotional or Bible reading guides, but when I got away from that I found myself digging more in the Word and really feasting on it. If one of those guides helps you though, then that's great. I just find they were a crutch to me because if I read through it, I felt like I was done. Really I knew in my heart that I should have dug a little deeper, read a little more, and reflected a little more on whatever passage it was.

When it comes to Bible reading, I think we probably all need to try hard to bring up the amount of time we spend in God's Word no matter how we go about doing it; whether it is with a devotional reading guide, going through it a book at a time, or finding topics to study through the Bible.

Final Thoughts

I know at times I have tried to *fudge* to myself that I'm better at some of these areas in my Christian life than I really am. I know that I have a whole list of things to work on.

In reality *fudging* is just another word for lying. The dictionary definition is to "present or deal with (something) in a vague, noncommittal, or inadequate way, esp. so as to conceal the truth or mislead."

I think some of us try to adjust things. We have checked off a number of items to make us sound a little better than we really are. We stack things up under a column in our Christian living and don't really think about the specifics. But frankly, it all adds up or doesn't add up.

I mentioned earlier about election years. During those we hear all types of ads, polls, and numbers, but how are our numbers in Christian living stacking up? If you had to rely on your record as a Christian, would you vote for yourself? Would you say your priorities and numbers are where you'd like to see them? I know mine could use some work.

So, are you eating the *fudge*?

10

A RECIPE FOR FRIENDSHIP

*A man that hath friends must shew
himself friendly... Proverbs 18:24*

Friendships are wonderful gifts to our lives straight from God. There are several references to friendship in the Bible. I think of the relationship of David and Jonathan (1 Samuel 18-20, 2 Samuel 1). Those chapters in Samuel are great reading. Jonathan and David had a great love and respect for each other.

I think of how in the Bible God called Abraham, "friend" (James 2:23). Moses also comes to mind. Remember God spoke to him, "face to face, as a man speaketh to his friend" (Exodus 33:11).

When it comes to our sisters in Christ, friendship takes on a special quality. Friendship between Christians is especially sweet because of the bond of Christ. We are enhanced by those special friendships. Building those strong friendships is a wonderful way to encourage and lift up others in the Lord.

Now the God of patience and consolation grant
you to be likeminded one toward another
according to Christ Jesus: That ye may with one
mind and one mouth glorify God, even the Father
of our Lord Jesus Christ. Romans 15:5-6

Bear ye one another's burdens, and so
fulfil the law of Christ. Galatians 6:2

Ointment and perfume rejoice the heart:
so doth the sweetness of a man's friend
by hearty counsel. Proverbs 27:9

Friends are one of the ways God takes care of us. We need all the things friendship entails from other human contact. We need the encouragement, the companionship, the love, the honesty, the loyalty, the understanding, and so many more things that it offers.

Our friendships with our sisters in Christ are like recipes of goodness for us. They bake up something special. You may have heard that saying, "In the cookies of life, friends are the chocolate chips". Friends are that sweet extra in life and even sweeter is friendship among believers in Christ.

Why is a recipe for fellowship and friendship with our sisters in Christ is so important? Let's check out the ingredients and see what they do.

Sisters In Christ Friendship Recipe

Shortening - Provides texture. Our fellowship and friendship with our sisters in the Lord can add much depth and texture to our lives. We blend together in unity as part of the body of Christ.

Sugar - Adds sweetness. Our fellowship with our sisters adds such a sweet taste to our lives. If we didn't have sugar in our cookies, we'd sure miss it. It is the same with our fellowship among our sisters. We can't leave it out of our lives.

Eggs - Holds the ingredients all together. Sisters in

the Lord are towers to lean on. We are held together by fellowship with them. We are stronger because of them, their prayers, and their love in the Lord. We have a special bond in Christ.

Vanilla - Adds flavor. Sisters add that flavor we need. They give us that extra sensation. Without friends and fellowship, we become kind of bland.

Flour - Adds substance. We need the substance a sister in the Lord can add. They give us many things by way of mentoring us when we don't even know it. Their shared testimonies inspire us. The way they live their lives has an impact on us.

Baking Soda - Leavens. Leavening agents in baking help to lighten the dough. Friendship with our sisters in Christ lightens our burdens through their prayer and encouragement.

Salt - Enhances flavor. Friendships truly increase flavor. Just when we need it, they help improve the tastefulness and quality of our lives. Friends are the type of people that know just what we are going through and are there when we need them.

Semi-Sweet Chocolate Chips - The kind of chocolate chips we normally add to our cookies is semi-sweet. Our sister friends tell us what they feel and think and that's okay. They can be honest and truthful to us. "Iron sharpeneth iron" (Proverbs 27:17).

Nuts - These are optional. Just a little craziness in a sister friend is great! Sometimes a little zaniness in our friends can be just the ingredient we need.

Final Thoughts

Friendships take a lot of time and effort to bake up, but they are worth it when we sense that sweet aroma and special bond that they bring. Friends that have Jesus in common will have lasting relationships, not just here on earth, but will dwell with Christ together throughout eternity.

A man that hath friends must shew himself
friendly: and there is a friend that sticketh
closer than a brother. Proverbs 18:24

I wonder if I'm the type of friend that I should be to others, especially to my sisters in Christ. Am I doing all those things that I should be doing? Am I lifting burdens, adding flavor, helping hold things together with my prayers, and all those other things? I hope I can improve in this area.

So, is your life a good recipe for friendship?

11

THE SOUND OF MUSIC

But ye are a chosen generation, a royal
priesthood, an holy nation, a peculiar people;
that ye should shew forth the praises of him
who hath called you out of darkness into his
marvellous light: 1 Peter 2:9

Dig Deeper: Read 1 Peter chapter 2.

I always think we can learn from anywhere, even a movie. It isn't always the spiritual things that come along in our lives that can make us stop and think.

For this lesson I just want to share with you some quotes from one of my favorite movies, *The Sound of Music*.

No doubt most of you have seen *The Sound of Music*, but have you ever noticed how much common sense is packed in there among the dialog and songs?

Here are some things that have struck me.

Climb every mountain.

Do all you are capable of doing. As a Christian, use your full potential. Keep reaching new heights. We have to keep climbing those mountains if we are ever going to accomplish anything for Christ.

Ford every stream.

Bear up under your burdens. Learn to rely on the Lord to give you strength. It will make it easier to cross the difficult parts of life.

Follow every rainbow.

Count your blessings. Don't forget to see the rainbows in the sky. Don't let life get you so down that you forget about those blessings that are right in front of you.

When you know the notes to sing, you can sing most anything.

Learn to be better. The more you know how to do something, the better you will become at it. As a Christian, we need to grab on to the Word and really take in all it can offer us to improve our walk for the Lord.

Nothing comes from nothing. Nothing ever could.

Don't expect anything without working. We can't expect our Christian walk to get to the level we need if we don't work at it. We have to put in some time to improving ourselves such as Bible study and prayer. We have to learn what it means to live holy lives.

When the Lord closes a door, somewhere He opens a window.

Look for opportunities. We can't get down when we get blocked from doing something, even if we think it was our way to serve the Lord. He may have a better way.

Be willing to be sensitive to the Lord's leading and find those opportunities of service. Those open windows of opportunity are out there. We just have to look for them.

Final Thoughts

I guess one of the reasons I like *The Sound of Music* so much is that it is all about music. Music has a way of capturing your heart.

I think our Christian lives should touch others like music. We should be fine-tuned. We should cause others joy. We should be that spark that gets someone moving. We should be that encourager. We should be that prayer warrior.

We don't want to be the discourager, the complainer, or the downer. That is not the sound of music. Rather, it is a screeching, grating, horrible sound.

The entire chapter of 1 Peter 2 is talking about getting our act in gear as a Christian. In verse 21 it mentions how we should follow Christ as our example.

We should be that beautiful music that is brought back into the house. Do you remember in *The Sound of Music*, when Captain Vonn Trapp says to Maria, "You brought music back into the house. I had forgotten."?

Do you need music brought back into your own house? Do you need to bring that joy of serving Christ back into your life? Our lives have to honor Christ in order to be that lovely sound to share with the world.

If we look in verse 9 of 1 Peter 2, it talks about how we should be a different kind of people because we are of Christ.

But ye are a chosen generation, a royal
priesthood, an holy nation, a peculiar people;
that ye should shew forth the praises of him who hath
called you out of darkness into his marvellous light.

How much do we do that? We have got to get out there and serve the Lord by climbing those mountains, fording those streams, counting our blessings, building our faith, and looking for those opportunities of service. We have to improve ourselves and be all we can to make that beautiful music as a Christian.

So, are you the sound of music?

12

BRANDED

*What? know ye not that your body is the temple of
the Holy Ghost which is in you, which ye have of
God, and ye are not your own? 1 Corinthians 6:19*

I have always been fascinated by the *Old West*. I
love all those old westerns with the shoot-outs and
cattle drives. I was thinking about those cowboys on
their cattle drives recently and about the concept of
branding. Branding was originally any visible mark
that showed identification for livestock.

When we become Christians, we are in a sense
branded for Christ. He sets His mark on us and sets
us apart. When we accept Christ as our personal
Savior, He has ownership of our bodies and us.
Come saddle up with me as we explore this concept
using some of the objects found in the Old West.

Horseshoe
The main purpose of a horseshoe is to furnish
protection for the horses' hooves against abrasion

77

and breakage. The Lord doesn't just set us in the world and expect us to have all the friction and roughness of the world bear into us as we bump along in life. The Lord is there to protect us. The world doesn't have that strong arm to lean on, but we do have Christ to lean on as children of the Lord. That is one thing that sets us apart.

The LORD is my light and my salvation; whom shall I fear? the LORD is the strength of my life; of whom shall I be afraid? When the wicked, even mine enemies and my foes, came upon me to eat up my flesh, they stumbled and fell. Though an host should encamp against me, my heart shall not fear: though war should rise against me, in this will I be confident. Psalm 27:1-3

He brought me up also out of an horrible pit, out of the miry clay, and set my feet upon a rock, and established my goings. Psalm 40:2

Chaps

Chaps were leather coverings for the legs of the cowboy. They were usually made out of sturdy leather and made to protect the legs. Modern cowboys sometimes still wear them. It was something that was needed in the Old West because of the shrubs and vegetation that tore at the cowboys legs. God gives us wonderful protection by providing His Word for us as His children.

When the world starts tearing at us and reaching out to grab us with all it has to offer, we can be refreshed and cling to the Word of God and find peace and comfort there. This sets us apart as Christians. Those without Christ don't have the comfort of God's Word to rely on.

This is my comfort in my affliction: for thy word hath quickened me. Psalm 119:50

My soul cleaveth unto the dust: quicken thou me according to thy word. Psalm 119:25

Cowboy Hat

The cowboy hat was used for protection from the sun, but it was also useful and functional to the cowboy. On their cattle drives the cowboys could signal with their hat and also use it to dip water out of streams when they were thirsty.

It is such a wonderful thing that the Lord is always there to shade us if we just stay close to Him. We can be shaded and dip into His Word and into the power of prayer and be refreshed in Him.

He that dwelleth in the secret place of the most High shall abide under the shadow of the Almighty. Psalm 91:1

Saddle

Saddles were originally used for working cattle ranchers. As Christians, we are set apart to work. We have a job to do. We are not set apart to be idle, but we are here to carry out the Great Commission.

God sets us apart from the world by making us His ambassadors. We represent Him. We need to be in the saddle so to speak, evangelizing and spreading the gospel and the love of Christ in our daily lives.

And he said unto them, Go ye into all the world, and preach the gospel to every creature. Mark 16:15

By this shall all men know that ye are my disciples,
if ye have love one to another. John 13:35

Tumbleweed

Tumbleweeds are plants that were abundant in the Old West. Now they are kept under control for the most part. If you live in the Western United States you may be familiar with them. They are plants that break away from their roots.

The wind can pick them up and carry them with great force, usually carrying lots of dust as they go. Tumbleweeds can be troublesome because they tend to push other vegetation out and take over.

The interesting thing about tumbleweeds is that they carry seeds everywhere when the wind blows them and more grow. They typically have around 250,000 seeds. They don't all scatter in one spot as tumbleweeds don't release all their seeds at once.

Isn't that so like the fiery darts of the devil? They keep on growing and coming at us as Christians.

The Lord knew that the tumbleweeds of the world would come rolling by in our lives as His children. Those tumbleweeds make us rely on Him more. The world doesn't have that reliance on the Lord like Christians do when tumbleweeds come. Having the knowledge that God is completely in control of every situation is something that sets us apart as Christians.

For I know the thoughts that I think toward you, saith the LORD, thoughts of peace, and not of evil, to give you an expected end. Jeremiah 29:11

And we know that all things work together for good to them that love God, to them who are the called according to his purpose. Romans 8:28

Spurs

If you are not familiar with what a spur is; it is a sharp metal piece attached to a cowboy boot. A spur is used for the purpose of goading a horse. It's an incentive to make the horse move forward. Christ left us with the Holy Spirit to be our spur.

The Holy Spirit is there to prick and guide us as Christians. When we are sensitive to His leading, we move forward in the direction that the Lord would have us go. This sets us apart as Christians. The world doesn't have the Holy Spirit to guide and direct them.

> *But the Comforter, which is the Holy Ghost, whom the Father will send in my name, he shall teach you all things, and bring all things to your remembrance, whatsoever I have said unto you. John 14:26*

> *Now the God of hope fill you with all joy and peace in believing, that ye may abound in hope, through the power of the Holy Ghost. Romans 15:13*

Final Thoughts

I love the fact that the Lord brands us with His touch. There is so much He gives us as His children. The things mentioned above are just a small helping of what God gives us when we accept Him as Lord of our lives.

Have you heard this saying before? *It's not important who you are, but Whose you are.*

There is so much we are given when we become Christians, but we have to remember *Whose* we are.

We have to live our lives according to how the Lord would have us because "we are not our own" as it states in 1 Corinthians 6:19.

I wonder if I stand out and people can see Whose brand is on me. As Christians, we are to shine in a dark world. I hope I'm doing that. I want to be identified for Christ.

So, *Whose* brand are you wearing?

13

I SAW 7 SHIPS COME SAILING BY

I will instruct thee and teach thee in the
way which thou shalt go: I will guide
thee with mine eye. Psalm 32:8

When I was growing up I used to love all those old movies that revolved around ships on the high seas. You know, like *Mutiny on the Bounty,* and some of those that had a little swashbuckling thrown in them.

Did you know we have our own *ships* that we are responsible for sailing through life?

(1) **Citizenship**

You've got have your papers to get on board!

Do you know Christ personally? Is your name written in the Book of Life? If you have accepted Christ, your citizenship is in heaven.

For our conversation is in heaven; from whence
also we look for the Saviour... Philippians 3:20

(2) **Ambassadorship**

We have our orders!

When we are a child of God, we become an ambassador for Christ. How well is this ship sailing for you? The mission of this ship is to represent Christ in how we live and in the spreading of His love and the message of the Gospel.

Now then we are ambassadors for Christ, as though God did beseech you by us: we pray you in Christ's stead, be ye reconciled to God. For he hath made him to be sin for us, who knew no sin; that we might be made the righteousness of God in him. 2 Corinthians 5:20-21

(3) **Friendship**

Heave! Ho!

Friendships takes a little work but boy are they worth the effort. It's not always calm waters, but having friends on the journey sure makes it more enjoyable.

Two are better than one; because they have a good reward for their labour. For if they fall,

the one will lift up his fellow: but woe to him
that is alone when he falleth; for he hath not
another to help him up. Ecclesiastes 4:9-10

Faithful are the wounds of a friend; but the
kisses of an enemy are deceitful. Proverbs 27:6

Ointment and perfume rejoice the heart:
so doth the sweetness of a man's friend
by hearty counsel. Proverbs 27:9

(4) **Fellowship**

All hands on deck!

Working together in unity helps this ship sail along. This ship is essential for our Christian life. We need our brothers and sisters in Christ. We depend on each other for prayer, encouragement, and to move forward to build up the Kingdom of God.

And they continued stedfastly
in the apostles' doctrine and
fellowship, and in breaking of
bread, and in prayers. Acts 2:42

If there be therefore any consolation in Christ,
if any comfort of love, if any fellowship of the Spirit,
if any bowels and mercies, Fulfil ye my joy, that
ye be likeminded, having the same love, being of one
accord, of one mind. Let nothing be done through
strife or vainglory; but in lowliness of mind let each
esteem other better than themselves. Look not every
man on his own things, but every man also on the
things of others. Philippians 2:1-4

(5) **Relationship**

Steady at the helm!

Our relationships with other people is something we all have to work on. I've already mentioned friendship and Christian fellowship, but those other relationships such as with our spouse, children, relatives, neighbors, and co-workers all need attention.

Each of these relationships have some intricate blueprints. All the mechanisms are different and sensitive for each. They operate in unique ways, so watch out how you steer and treat these ships. Pay attention to them and keep them fine-tuned or a gasket may blow!

...Thou shalt love thy neighbour as thyself.
Matthew 22:39

And the Lord make you to increase and
abound in love one toward another, and
toward all men... 1 Thessalonians 3:12

Therefore all things whatsoever ye would that
men should do to you, do ye even so to them:
for this is the law and the prophets. Matthew 7:12

There are several passages throughout the Scripture that refer to our relationships with our parents, children, and spouses, and I'm not going to list them out here, but working on each relationship is important.

Taking time to really evaluate where you are in your relationship with each might help you to take some steps to improve those relationships and sail along a little more smoothly.

(6) Discipleship

Make way for the Captain!

At times when Christ was teaching His disciples,

they were on a ship. Remember Peter's lesson about faith? It's scary to get out of the boat and test the waters. Isn't it?

How about when they had fished all night and caught nothing? Then Jesus had them go out into the deep and lower the nets.

Look at the amazing thing that happened when they did as Jesus asked. They caught so many fish the net broke.

Now when he had left speaking, he said unto Simon, Launch out into the deep, and let down your nets for a draught. And Simon answering said unto him, Master we have toiled all the night, and have taken nothing: nevertheless at thy word I will let down the net. And when they had this done, they inclosed a great multitude of fishes: and their net brake. Luke 5:4-6

There is also the time Christ was out on a ship with the disciples and was asleep when the storm came up. They learned another lesson about faith that day.

And there arose a great storm of wind, and the waves beat into the ship, so that it was now full. And he was in the hinder part of the ship, asleep on a pillow: and they awake him, and say unto him, Master, carest thou not that we perish? And he arose, and rebuked the wind, and said unto the sea, Peace, be still. And the wind ceased, and there was a great calm. And he said unto them, Why are ye so fearful? how is it that ye have no faith? And they feared exceedingly, and said one to another, What manner of man is this, that even the wind and the sea obey him? Mark 4:37-41

Being a disciple doesn't mean there is always going to be smooth sailing, but we know the Maker of those waves. We've just got to follow Him and listen to Him and do as He commands us to do.

It requires getting into the Word and getting to know the Lord and what He expects of us in order to follow Him. We are to live to reflect Christ.

...If ye continue in my word, then are ye my disciples indeed; John 8:31

By this shall all men know that ye are my disciples, if ye have love one to another. John 13:35

Herein is my Father glorified, that ye bear much fruit; so shall ye be my disciples. John 15:8

(7) **Worship**

Pipe down!

That is a nautical term that means the pipe has blown and it's time for lights out and to be quiet on the ship. My dad used to say that to us when I was growing up, but I never knew where the saying came from until recently.

There are some times we have just got to pipe down and do what Psalm 46:10 says,

Be still, and know that I am God...

It is essential that our worship sails correctly or we'll find we are sinking fast in our Christian life. Without worship we get punctures and leaks in our very lining. When we get our eyes off of the Lord, worldly and ungodly influences will come rushing into our lives with a force that you won't believe.

It is not just that Sunday morning worship either, although that's important, but to daily communicate with the Lord, read His Word, pray, and really reflect on Who God is sums up our worship.

*Give unto the LORD the glory due unto his name;
worship the LORD in the beauty of holiness. Psalm 29:2*

Final Thoughts

Here we are out on the high seas of the waters of life and we need to have our ships going in the right direction. Once we have got that *citizenship* (Salvation) in order, the rest of those ships need to be watched and maintained.

We've got to batten down the hatches because there are so many dangers out there. The waters can be deep, the wind might not always be on our side, and what about those pesky pirates?

Pirates come in several forms, sneaking over the side our of our ships with their grimy faces, steely eyes, and menacing smiles. Sometimes we see their black flags raised and know they're coming and sometimes they catch us off guard.

They may creep up in the form of challenges that come up in our lives, the weight of heavy schedules, and even just the everyday journey of life that makes us feel like they've got us cornered to walk the plank.

When we feel like that, maybe we need to step back and reflect. Get out on deck and feel the salty air and take a deep breath. Look around and out upon the horizon.

God made that wonderful sea of life and with the Lord as your Captain you can have such a fulfilling journey. Talk about a *Master and Commander*!

...even the winds and the sea obey him! Matthew 8:27

Let the Lord be your guide. Use His Word as your compass to align your ships in the right direction, and really work on the fleet you've been entrusted with.

*I will instruct thee and teach thee in the
way which thou shalt go: I will guide thee
with mine eye. Psalm 32:8*

So, how are your ships sailing?

14

ENCOURAGING WORDS

And when Asa heard these words, and the prophecy
of Obed the prophet, he took courage...   2 Chronicles 15:8

I was reading through 2 Chronicles 15 not long ago, and although I've read that passage many times concerning Asa, it really stuck me that he "took courage" only "when" he heard the words of Azariah and Obed the prophet.

It made me want to look back over what was actually said to Asa in order to see what made him "take courage".

As I read and reread those verses it occurred to me that what was said to Asa is such a good pattern for us as we deal with people that are discouraged and down in their Christian life.

Not only can we encourage others, we can encourage ourselves with these things that Azariah, the son of Obed reminded Asa of in this passage.

Let's take a look at how Asa was encouraged when he needed it.

First, Asa was reminded of God's presence.

And he went out to meet Asa, and said
unto him, Hear ye me, Asa, and all
Judah and Benjamin; The LORD
is with you... 2 Chronicles 15:2

What a great reminder for all of us that, hey! God is with us. It's so fitting that Azariah starts out with such a powerful thought such as the reminder of God's presence.

When I'm discouraged I always enjoy meditating on Psalm 91. Those verses are full of little reminders that God is with us. It's a great encouragement to me.

Second, Asa was reminded to seek the Lord.

...The LORD is with you, while ye be with
him; and if ye seek him, he will be found
of you; but if ye forsake him, he will
forsake you. 2 Chronicles 15:2

What great advice. We all know we need to seek

the Lord, but sometimes we need a gentle reminder to do just that.

Next, Asa was reminded of God's power.

Now for a long season Israel hath been without the true God, and without a teaching priest, and without law. But when they in their trouble did turn unto the LORD God of Israel, and sought him, he was found of them. And in those times there was no peace to him that went out, nor to him that came in, but great vexations were upon all the inhabitants of the countries. And nation was destroyed of nation, and city of city: for God did vex them with all adversity. 2 Chronicles 15:3-6

In these verses Asa is reminded of what God can do. When I'm discouraged I know that is one of the things that seems to really help me.

Just thinking back on all that God has done for me personally and the ways that He's moved in my life revives me. It is such a spirit lifter and motivator.

We see that Azariah reminded Aza and all the

people that were there with him of how God worked in the past with power concerning Israel.

Lastly, Asa was reminded to be strong.

Be ye strong therefore, and let not your
hands be weak: for your work shall
be rewarded. 2 Chronicles 15:7

Wow! That was such a great way to top things off. It was like whip cream on top of a piece of pie. Azariah was telling Asa to just be strong. Just hang in there.

Those are such motivating words in verse seven of that chapter.

One of the verses that comes to my mind when things get rough is Ephesians 6:10

Finally, my brethren, be strong in the
Lord, and in the power of his might.

That verse always inspires me to just keep on keeping on.

Final Thoughts

Azariah not only excited Asa to "take courage" but his words of reminder also spurred Asa into action. In 2 Chronicles 15:8, it says that Asa removed the idols and also that he "renewed the altar of the LORD".

As the passage goes on it talks about what the people did when they saw what Asa had done. I encourage you to read through 2 Chronicles 15:9-15. We see in those verses that not only did Asa take action, but his actions motivated others to action as well.

It says in verse 11, after the people saw that God was with Asa, the people offered an offering to the Lord of their spoil. In verse 12, it says that the people entered into a covenant with the Lord.

You'll notice that it wasn't halfway actions either, but the covenant they entered into was with all their heart and with all their soul.

In verse 15, it says that they "sought him [the LORD] with their whole desire".

Sometimes all it takes to lift up another brother

or sister in Christ is just some encouraging words. I wonder how many people I encourage with my words? How many people do I build up and then energize into action in their service to the Lord by what I say?

I think that the reminders that were given to Asa are some good things to use to encourage others and ourselves as well.

So, are your words encouraging?

15
ULTIMATE SURVIVAL

Wherefore take unto you the whole armour
of God, that ye may be able to withstand in the evil
day, and having done all, to stand. Ephesians 6:13

Many of us have seen television survival shows. Those are there to entertain us, but the Christian life is not entertainment. It is the real survival course.

It is a course that doesn't just last only a few weeks or months, but once we become a child of God, it is how we live. The Christian walk is how we survive this world below until the Lord returns for us.

Yes, there are dangers and challenges out there! The Bible says,

Be sober, be vigilant; because your adversary
the devil, as a roaring lion, walketh about,
seeking whom he may devour: 1 Peter 5:8

This is not to say that God doesn't equip us, but He does want us to know what we are up against.

For we wrestle not against flesh and blood,
But against principalities, against powers, against
the rulers of the darkness of this world, against
spiritual wickedness in high places. Ephesians 6:12

God loves us and gives us all the directions and equipment we need for our survival. Read through Ephesians 6:10-18, and you'll see everything that's needed. We have to put on our survival gear!

Strong (Ephesians 6:10)

First of all, we need to be "strong in the Lord" Don't forget! We have God Almighty to lean on for our survival. So many people quip off the pieces of our Christian armor without this point, but it is important to be strong as we put on those individual pieces of armor.

Truth (Ephesians 6:14)

Next, we need to have our "loins girt about with truth". When we protect our loins we are protecting our midriff or sensitive areas. We can only do this with truth.

Righteousness (Ephesians 6:14)

Wear the "breastplate of righteousness". This can only be done by making sure we have a daily relationship with God. We have to keep our lives holy.

Gospel of Peace (Ephesians 6:15)

Have your "feet shod with the preparation of the gospel of peace". How can we survive if we do not have our feet planted firmly and surefooted for stability?

Shield of Faith (Ephesians 6:16)

Look at the importance that is put on this one. The verse says, "Above all, taking the shield of faith". The shield in our armor is something that we hold up to ward off the attacks of the enemy. It is a necessity to answer all of the adversity that we come in contact with in this life.

Helmet of Salvation (Ephesians 6:17)

"And take the helmet of salvation". If we don't

wear our helmet, then we don't have anything to protect our head! Remembering our Salvation can help us ward off bad thinking and distressing thoughts that can target us and get us down.

Sword of the Spirit (Ephesians 6:17)

"And take the sword of the Spirit" Our sword is the Word of God. This is a weapon that we need to get skillful at using.

God's Word was the weapon that Jesus used when the devil came to tempt Him. We have to have it in our hearts in order to use it for our survival.

Praying Always (Ephesians 6:18)

"Praying always with all prayer and supplication in the Spirit". Not only are we told what armor to wear, but also we are told what our stance should be.

Part of our survival depends on our praying with sensitivity toward the Spirit, which can only come about by living holy lives.

Watching (Ephesians 6:18)

"Watching thereunto with all perseverance and supplication for all saints". We cannot survive alone. Our very survival is entangled with other Christians.

We should look out for other Christians, work and fellowship together, and keep them in our prayers.

<u>Final Thoughts</u>

To survive this world and all it has to throw at us, we need to learn to have some good survival skills. We ought to work at it. We ought to see the need to hone those skills.

It's so important that we learn to use and wear our armor that is already provided for us in Ephesians 6. It helps us to hold on. It helps us to endure. It helps us carry on and keep on going.

**So, did you remember to put
your armor on today?**

16

ALL COOKIED UP

But the fruit of the Spirit is love, joy, peace,
longsuffering, gentleness, goodness, faith,
Meekness, temperance: against such there
is no law. Galatians 5:22-23

Potatoes come in a lot of varieties from the white, red, fingerling, to the Russet, and a few more. Plus they can all be cooked in various ways. As Christians, we can be "cooked" in a lot of different ways as well.

The choices we make in life will help form how we turn out in the end. We want our choices to reflect all that Fruit of the Spirit that Galatians 5 talks about, so we have to be careful and not get "cooked" in the wrong way.

Don't get scalloped.

Scalloping a dish requires us to put whatever we are using in some kind of sauce, like that rich, creamy, cheesy sauce we use for scalloped potatoes.

What about us? What have we been immersed in? Is it the love of God? Have we spent time with the Lord before we go about our day, or are we dripping with bad attitudes and hateful temperaments?

When we scallop something, it normally forms that crusty goodness on top, like on scalloped potatoes of which I am a fan. That crustiness is great on potatoes, but not on people. Have you developed a callousness to your shell? Do you say crusty words? Get a little grumpy?

Let all bitterness, and wrath, and anger, and
clamour, and evil speaking, be put away from you,
with all malice: And be ye kind one to another,
tenderhearted, forgiving one another, even as God
for Christ's sake hath forgiven you. Ephesians 4:31-32

Don't get boiled.

Boiling water is fantastic for cooking potatoes, but boiling doesn't bode so well for Christians. We are not to get boiling mad. Got a red face with smoke billowing out your ears? There are so many

verses concerning anger in the Bible. Look what it
says in Ephesians 4:26.

Be ye angry, and sin not: let not the
sun go down upon your wrath.

Don't get mashed.

Are you one of those Christians that have gotten
mashed? Do you feel discouraged? Allowed the
mixers and beaters of the world to get you down?
Pressed down about as far as you feel you can go?

It's easy to get that way. We all have times when
we get down, but we have to work on not allowing it
to happen and not allowing ourselves to stay down
once we are. We have to reach to the Lord to get
back up and find our joy in Him. We have to rely on
His strength and not our own.

I can do all things through Christ which
strengtheneth me. Philippians 4:13

Don't get baked.

I enjoy a baked potato. Sometimes when I'm in a

hurry I put them in the microwave, but there is just something about those potatoes that have actually baked in the oven.

Again, the process of baking is great for potatoes, but not for Christians. We can get burnt. Do we allow ourselves to get baked in the world? Do we allow what's out there to affect us? Do we need to change our choice of tv shows, books, magazines, or friends? When the heat of the world seeps in, it can get baked right into us until people can't even tell we are Christians.

I beseech you therefore, brethren, by the mercies of God, that ye present your bodies a living sacrifice, holy, acceptable unto God, which is your reasonable service. And be not conformed to this world: but be ye transformed by the renewing of your mind, that ye may prove what is that good, and acceptable, and perfect, will of God. Romans 12:1-2

Don't get fried.

When I was little my mom fried potatoes a lot. She would always fry them in a cast iron skillet and get it really hot with a little oil. Mmm. They were always so good.

Potatoes can survive the heat and the oil, but when we go dipping our feet into the vat of sin, we can really end up hurting ourselves. The burn of sin scars us. Sure, the Lord forgives us if we ask Him, but there are always going to be consequences to our sin.

The consequences of our sin may not just affect us and our testimony for the Lord, but sometimes splatters out of the skillet and onto our family and other relationships. Sin clogs up our lives.

Be not deceived; God is not mocked: for whatsoever a man soweth, that shall he also reap. For he that soweth to his flesh shall of the flesh reap corruption; but he that soweth to the Spirit shall of the Spirit reap life everlasting. Galatians 6:7-8

Final Thoughts

Life boils down to the choices we make, and as Christians we have to be so careful or we end up being "cooked" in ways that we don't want to be.

We just have to be diligent about how we go about every single day. We have to allow ourselves to be *cooked* up in ways that glorify the Lord.

We have to choose to be that *sweet* potato. How can we show the love of Christ if we're running around with crusty attitudes, are ill tempered, have steam coming out of our ears, are discouraged, or have become worldly Christians? We are to be Christ-like.

I am crucified with Christ: nevertheless I live; yet not I, but Christ liveth in me: and the life which I now live in the flesh I live by the faith of the Son of God, who loved me, and gave himself for me. Galatians 2:20

But the fruit of the Spirit is love, joy, peace, longsuffering, gentleness, goodness, faith, Meekness, temperance: against such there is no law. Galatians 5:22-23

I know I'm not always a "sweet" potato. There is always something I need to work on.

So, how are you cooked?

17
CRUSHED

*We are troubled on every side, yet not
distressed; we are perplexed, but not in despair;
Persecuted, but not forsaken; cast down, but
not destroyed; 2 Corinthians 4:8-9*

Over the years of working with women's ministry and having a website online for so many years, I have heard from hundreds of hurting women and continue to hear from them. Some of these ladies are not just hurting, but *crushed.*

Our church women's groups probably all have at least one crushed woman in them and some groups may have several. Circumstances have beaten these women down. Many women have heavy loads they have to bear. A rough life can take a toll on anyone no matter how tough they are.

Our churches have all kinds of programs for these women; classes for the abused, programs for those needing assistance, and all kinds of things. I think that is all well and good, but I think we forget where some of the biggest help is to getting out from under a heavy load. That is the help found in God's Word. We have to allow the Word to help lift our burdens.

We need to teach women to memorize God's Word, to respect it, to hang on to it. Scripture can ease the pain that life has stacked on top of us.

I know when life gets me down I always have God's Word ready and handy to pull out of my memory. What is sad is that all Christian women can't say that. Sure, I learned a lot of that Scripture when I was a kid, but I have to keep learning even though I am over fifty.

Yes, it is harder when we are older. Our brains are not as quick with putting things to memory. But it is not just memory, we can retain so much just by studying and getting into the Word of God and reading it.

We are supposed to be diligent and study God's Word (2 Timothy 2:15), hide it in our hearts (Psalms 119:11), write it on our walls (Deuteronomy 6:7-9), and desire it (1 Peter 2:2).

Our women's ministries should be a place where we are encouraging women to hold on to Scripture. Life can be hard at times for many of us, but think how hard it is for Christian women who do not know God's Word. We have to teach them to hang on to Scripture.

I have found that it is not even a matter of how long a woman has known the Lord. I see more and more that even women that have been Christians for years have really not gotten the basic Scriptures and doctrines under their belt.

We can blame it on our churches. We can blame it on our pastors. We can blame it on our women's ministries. It doesn't really matter why. It just needs to change.

We need to teach women to learn the Bible, to hone in on studying, memorizing, and having a desire for the Word of God. Then when life comes knocking hard and crushing them, they have Scripture to cling to.

Here are some of my favorite passages to go to when I feel crushed.

Psalm 91	Matthew 11:28-30
Psalm 37:1-4	Joshua 1:9
Romans 15:13	Philippians 4:13

Final Thoughts

Sure, we are all going to have times when we feel crushed and have some heavy burdens to bear. Each of us will have these times on different scales, but no matter what the degree of our burden, we should be able to ease that crushed feeling when we get into the Word of God and soak it in for a while.

It doesn't matter whether our burdens are on the epic proportion that Job faced or the little worries that weigh on us daily, the Lord will be there for us to lift us up and carry us through.

We are troubled on every side, yet not distressed; we are perplexed, but not in despair; persecuted, but not forsaken; cast down, but not destroyed; 2 Corinthians 4:8-9

So, where do you turn when you feel crushed?

18

MAKE LIFE BEARABLE

Bear ye one another's burdens, and so
fulfil the law of Christ. Galatians 6:2

Bearing the burdens of each other is a big part of our Christian lives. It should be something that we do, not just because the Bible tells us, although that is important, but we should see the need to do it.

We all have burdens to bear at one time or another and we all know how being in that place calls for relief. We might not all face the same type of burdens or even the same weight of burdens, but we all have them in one shape or form.

As humans, we should be sensitive to others that have heavy burdens to bear. As Christians, it is even more important. We need to learn to B-E-A-R.

(B) Brunt
(E) Empathy
(A) Afflictions
(R) Responsibilities

Bear the brunt.

Have you ever been faced with a burden to bear and you felt like you were weak in the knees because it was so heavy? I think anyone feels that way when they go through a trial, especially when it first hits them. When you feel the brunt of a trial, you feel all that force and impact. You just want a little of that weight off of your shoulders.

The doorbell or the phone ringing can sometimes strike fear in a person when they have a heavy burden, because when you are that low, you just don't want to deal with anyone or anything. I think that is where we can step in. We can help someone out by just answering the door or the phone for them, taking messages, or fielding questions.

Just doing any little thing to help can take the brunt of the impact off of the person going through the hard time. Stepping in and helping to alleviate unnecessary weight on someone that is already feeling beaten down can ease some of that forceful impact that has struck at them. We can act as a shield to those people. We can help soften the blow.

Bear with empathy.

Empathy is basically just an understanding of how someone else is feeling, and when you have a friend or loved one going through a rough time, they want to know that you understand.

You may just need to stop and listen to them. You might not even have to talk at all. Maybe just be there to give them a hug or hold their hand. From time to time we all need someone who just says, "I'm here for you".

Hurting people just want to know someone else is there for them and that someone else is in their corner. Sometimes we have to feel a little bit of their pain too.

Bear up afflictions.

I don't like afflictions but I've had my share. It can be any burden you have to carry or any situation that hurts you to go through. Hurting people are vulnerable people because their defenses are down. They need some lifting up. One way to do that is to pray for them. Sounds basic, but praying for others is such an important part of our Christian living.

Encouraging them in other ways can really help too. Maybe it is just a simple card you send that says you are thinking of them. Maybe it is a phone call or even a text message to say they are in your prayers. There are all kinds of ways to say you care and want to help in any given situation.

Bear the responsibilities.

When you are the person hurting, you aren't in a vacuum. Life goes on without you. Maybe you have kids or a husband who still has to get up and go to school or work every day. Everything keeps moving along at a fast pace and you are in slow pace mode.

Some things just naturally have to slide in your everyday routine. You may not be up to doing normal everyday tasks, whether you are dealing with a physical burden, or whether you just are so low that you don't have the strength to carry on.

Helping out with responsibilities is another place that we all can step in and help someone in this situation. Can we pick up the kids from school? Do their laundry? Make them a meal? Pick up the dry cleaning? Go to the grocery store? Maybe even walk the dog?

We all have responsibilities. Life is full of little details and everyday jobs that still need to get done even when we aren't feeling up to it.

As Christians, we should want to dive right in to help ease the burdens of everyday life for someone else.

Final Thoughts

I've had times in my life, like after surgery, or when I was just going a rough time, where I've had some wonderful Christian people and friends at my side. I'm not sure what I would have done without them. They lifted me up when I was down.

People that help bear the burdens of others are such an encouragement. Just being there and acting as a friend can make all the difference in the world.

I found a quote from one of my favorite bears and his little friend. I like what Piglet says to Winnie-the-Pooh. It says a lot.

"I don't feel very much like Pooh today," said Pooh.
"There there," said Piglet. "I'll bring you tea and honey until you do." (A.A. Milne, Winnie-the-Pooh)

So, are you bearing the burdens of others?

19

INSIDE MY POCKETS

Prove all things; hold fast that
which is good. 1 Thessalonians 5:21

Pockets are useful things. Sometimes we keep things in our pockets for safe keeping. Other times it is just convenience.

When my son was little I can remember finding Legos and small dinosaurs in his pockets when I'd do the laundry. He seemed to have a knack for putting small toys in his pockets when he was little. It didn't even matter if it was a little pocket, he'd find a way to stuff something in there.

I wonder what we'd find in our pockets if we looked close. You know—those hidden places in our lives that we keep safe from everyone else—those deep places that no one can see but us and God.

Precious in My Pocket

Have you ever used a pocket to carry something precious? I think of military men and women who carry photos of their loved ones with them in their pockets when they are deployed. It helps carry them through the road they have to travel.

As Christians, what do we carry with us because it is important?

The Blood of Christ

One thing I think about is the precious blood of Christ.

Forasmuch as ye know that ye were not redeemed with corruptible things, as silver and gold, from your vain conversation received by tradition from your fathers; But with the precious blood of Christ, as of a lamb without blemish and without spot: 1 Peter 1:18-19

That blood is what saves us. It covers our sins. Christ shed His blood for us. That fact should make us never want to lose sight of how precious Christ's blood is.

The blood of Christ to me is an overwhelming thing. It does so much. It cleanses, saves, sanctifies, redeems, heals, and so much more.

When the devil was cast out of heaven in Revelation 12, the blood is what brought him down. It is what overcame him (Revelation 12:9-11).

The Promise of Christ's Return

Think about the promise of Christ's return that we get to carry with us all the time. It is a wonderful possession and we should hold tight to it.

Let not your heart be troubled: ye believe in God, believe also in me. In my Father's house are many mansions: if it were not so, I would have told you. I go to prepare a place for you. And if I go and prepare a place for you, I will come again, and receive you unto myself; that where I am, there ye may be also. John 14:1-3

Instruction

I guess we wouldn't get into so much trouble if we all remembered to keep what we have learned and have it handy to pull out and use when we need it, especially when it comes to wisdom, Bible verses, and Biblical instruction.

Take fast hold of instruction; let her not go:
keep her; for she is thy life. Proverbs 4:13

Righteousness

Look what Job said about his righteousness. He thought it was worth holding on to.

My righteousness I hold fast, and will not let it go: my
heart shall not reproach me so long as I live. Job 27:6

We need to let others do what they will, but we need to keep hold of living and doing right no matter what the circumstance.

Holes in My Pocket

None of us want holes in our pockets. They can make us lose things. What are you losing that is valuable?

Hope

Don't lose hope. Hope lifts us. Hope helps us hold on when it seems like things all around us are failing. It's a powerful thing so we want to keep it close and safe in our pocket.

Now our Lord Jesus Christ himself, and
God, even our Father, which hath loved us,
and hath given us everlasting consolation
and good hope through grace, Comfort your
hearts, and stablish you in every good word
and work. 2 Thessalonians 2:16-17

Faith

Don't lose your faith. Faith is something we need to carry with us. Without faith we are powerless.

Now faith is the substance of things hoped for,
the evidence of things not seen. Hebrews 11:1

Witness

Did you ever stop to consider you are carrying precious seed in your pocket?

He that goeth forth and weepeth, bearing
precious seed, shall doubtless come again
with rejoicing, bringing his sheaves
with him. Psalm 126:6

That seed should be important and valuable to us. We shouldn't do anything to lose that witness. Others are counting on us to have it with us. We are carrying something more precious than gold that we need to deliver.

Picked Pockets

There are some things that we carry with us that we allow circumstances or other people to just pick out of our pockets. What are you allowing to be picked from your pockets?

Joy

What about our joy? Do you ever allow others to steal your joy from you? Maybe it was some rough circumstance that sidled up next to you and the next thing you knew, your pockets were empty of joy. Joy is one of those things we need to keep safe and secure.

Rejoice in the Lord alway: and
again I say, Rejoice. Philippians 4:4

Confidence

Confidence is another thing that we may allow others to steal from us. I think sometimes we need to remember that we are God's children when something like that happens. Remembering we are a child of God bolsters us up.

Behold, what manner of love the Father
hath bestowed upon us, that we should
be called the sons of God... 1 John 3:1

Control

Another thing I think we are all guilty of at one time or another is allowing someone else to rob us of our control. Losing control is not a good thing, especially as a Christian. Losing control can harm our testimony for Christ. We have to keep control not only of our tongues, but of our behavior as a whole.

Whoso keepeth his mouth and his
tongue keepeth his soul from
troubles. Proverbs 21:23

He that hath no rule over his own spirit
is like a city that is broken down, and
without walls. Proverbs 25:28

When we lose things out of our pockets because of holes, it usually means that the stitching has come lose. You've probably heard that quote that says, *A day hemmed in prayer is less likely to unravel.* That is so true. We might need to do a little mending with some prayer and Bible study to keep our pockets shored up.

Hidden in my Pocket

Have you ever seen on reality police shows where people are pulled over and they have something illegal in their possession? The police always seem to find what those people try to hide hurriedly before they are stopped. I wonder what we as Christians have hiding in our pockets. If we had to fork it over, what would we pull out?

Would there be bitterness, unforgiveness, and maybe even some hardened anger stuck in our pockets? Those things are kind of hard to hide completely. They have a way of sticking out and will eventually show in how we talk and act.

Of course we know God sees the heart, but sometimes we try to hide things anyway. In reality we cannot hide anything from God.

This then is the message which we have heard of him, and declare unto you, that God is light, and in him is no darkness at all. If we say that we have fellowship with him, and walk in darkness, we lie, and do not the truth: But if we walk in the light, as he is in the light, we have fellowship one with another, and the blood of Jesus Christ his Son cleanseth us from all sin. If we say that we have no sin, we deceive ourselves, and the truth is not in us. If we confess our sins, he is faithful and just to forgive us our sins, and to cleanse us from all unrighteousness. If we say that we have not sinned, we make him a liar and his word is not in us. 1 John 1:5-10

Decoration on My Pocket

Some pockets have beautiful stitching on them. It may be pretty embroidered flowers. Other times it may be initials.

What decorates us? What do people see when they look at us? Do they see the Fruit of the Spirit? Do they see the love of Christ?

Initials on the pockets show ownership. Can people look at us and know we belong to Christ?

For we are his workmanship, created
in Christ Jesus unto good works, which
God hath before ordained that we should
walk in them. Ephesians 2:10

Hands in My Pockets

In the afternoons I stick my feet up for a few minutes before I need to start dinner and I watch *Judge Judy*. I just love it when someone puts their hands in their pockets when they are standing in her courtroom.

If you are an avid *Judge Judy* watcher, then you know that it doesn't go over very well. She says in her sharp voice, "Get your hands out of your pockets!" and then she proceeds with the rolling of the eyes. I always get a kick out of her reaction when someone has their hands in their pockets.

We definitely shouldn't have our hands in our pockets when it comes to the Christian life. There is work to be done. We can't be idle or lazy.

Say not ye, There are yet four months, and then cometh harvest? behold, I say unto you, Lift up your eyes, and look on the fields; for they are white already to harvest. John 4:35

Final Thoughts

I know I need to evaluate the things that I carry around with me. Perhaps I need to pretend it is laundry day and check my pockets. I want to go through life hanging a little tighter to the things that are important.

Maybe there are even some things I need to let go. It is so easy to get off course and allow things to filter in that just don't make a difference when it comes to eternity.

As it says in 1 Thessalonians 5:21,

Prove all things; hold fast that which is good.

So, what's in your pockets?

20

THAT STUFF ON OUR PLATE

Be still, and know that I am God: I will
be exalted among the heathen, I will be
exalted in the earth. Psalm 46:10

Have you ever uttered that phrase, "I've got too much stuff on my plate!"? What we mean is that our lives have become too busy.

It's funny that we teach our children not to take too much food, other than what they will eat, and not put too much "stuff" on their plates. Yet, here many of us are as adults with way too much stuff on our own plates.

We have allowed ourselves to be involved with so many things that it has the potential to hinder our well-being.

Personally, I enjoy being busy. I can't stand laziness, but sometimes we can become so busy that life seems to consume us. I don't think Christ intended us to live that way.

When we get in that all too familiar busy mode

of running, running, and running, we tend to let those nutritional things that should be on our plate slide off the side. We let things go by the wayside like our prayer and Bible study.

Sometimes if we do keep those things on our plate, we tend to treat them like salt and pepper, and only flavor our lives with them. We don't really have a full course meal of the things that can give us protein and help us survive.

Sometimes our family time slides off the side of our plate like runny gravy. It just starts dripping off and we barely even notice how far away from those around us we have become.

When we are in that busy mode, we tend to push aside those things that should be important. We don't mean to. We just start playing with our fork and it just happens.

I think it is a challenge to make ourselves have a balanced plate as a Christian, but I do think it is something we should strive for. It may be we need to just write out our schedule and see what we're actually spending time on. It may be we need to choose what are priorities and what are not. I'm sure for everybody there's a different way to go about it, but the need to keep Christ at the center of our lives is the key.

There are some things that I like to check up on once in a while just to be sure I'm on track. Sometimes these four areas of my life need my attention.

Relationships

How are my relationships with my husband, children, friends, and especially with the Lord?

Time

Where am I spending my time?

Activities

What all am I involved in? Is there too much?

Priorities

What are my priorities? Do I keep the important things where they should be?

Final Thoughts

I love that "be still" part of Psalm 46:10.

Be still and know that I am God... Psalm 46:10

Wow! That requires slowing down and just look at the benefits. Taking a much-needed break to reflect on God and His greatness, His love, His power will help us know Him.

Even in the midst of all that is going on around us, we need to take that time to spend with the Lord.

So, what's on your plate?

21

ON THE RIGHT TRACK!

Shew me thy ways, O LORD;
teach me thy paths. Psalms 25:4

This verse in Psalm 25 has always been one of my favorites over the years. Frankly, I need the Lord so much to help direct my paths and show me the way in my life.

When we are following those "paths" that it talks about, and seeking the Lord to guide us, we tend to be more joyful Christians. On the other hand, relying on the Lord to "teach" us His paths is what I think we all have trouble with though.

I look at it as kind of like following train tracks. The *Conductor* knows what's up ahead, but we may not. As humans, that great unknown scares us. At least it scares me.

Of course if we get off and start taking and making our own path, we get derailed and lose our way, and lose our focus in our Christian lives. We need to rely on the Lord daily in order to be where we need to be.

When I was little, I think in Kindergarten, our class went on a field trip to ride a train. I was raised near Marion, Ohio, and there are so many train tracks in that town that I guess a field trip to ride a train was a fitting thing to do.

I remember it being so exciting, although in reality I think they only took us about 10 or 15 feet for our ride. It was still fun.

I was thinking about that verse in Psalm 25:4, trains, and that field trip awhile back, and my mind went wandering to all things related to trains. The Christian life is about getting on the train, allowing the *Conductor* to take control, and not getting derailed.

Know God can.

Remember the story about *The Little Engine That Could*? When trying to go uphill, he kept saying, "I think I can!", "I think I can!". That's all well and good, but as Christians we can say, "I know God can!", "I know God can!". Through our faith we can use God's strength as we go up those hills of life.

Trains are strong.

Trains are usually made to be pretty strong and powerful. They have to be. Many of them carry cargo, go long distances, and need to get to where they are going with speed.

When we are relying on Christ, we can be pretty powerful too. We'll be able to bear the burdens that we have because we are letting the Lord carry them for us. We can move along the track in His strength instead of our own.

Ride the *I-Am-The Way-Trak*.

In the States, we all know what the *Amtrak* is. Its name is from "America" and "track" and it's that fast train that sails past us and carries passengers in quick time.

For Christians, we need to travel a different line, the "I-Am-The Way-Trak". Only Christ can guide us and show us the way. When we follow the Lord's leading instead of our own, we end up at the proper destination. Christ is the *Conductor*.

For some of us, we've developed our own line—the "Me-Trak". We want things our own way, and we can really start going in the wrong direction in our Christian lives when we start riding that one.

Trains require a source of energy.

There has got to be something that makes the train go. Older trains used coal to fire them up. Now it's mostly diesel-electric, but no matter what type of train, it needs something to power it.

For us, the Holy Spirit can be our power source. Being filled with the Spirit can spur us on and keep us fueled.

Keep chugging forward.

We don't see many trains moving backwards. All the wheels of a train have to move forward in order to get where it needs to be. The wheels need to be greased and oiled and in good working order in order to move and stop when the conductor wants the train to move and stop.

As a Christian, we need our daily tune up too. We need our prayer and Bible study so we are ready to move forward and follow the leading of our Conductor.

<u>Final Thoughts</u>

Sometimes it's hard living the Christian life and keeping on track. Our cargo bed gets bogged down with burdens and we forget to let Christ carry them.

We see a split in the tracks and sometimes don't know what direction to go, and believe me, crossroads can be scary. We get so busy with daily schedules that we seem like our wheels are spinning and that we are getting nowhere.

Sometimes we just need to remember Who our Conductor is—that He's that great *Power Source* that we need to keep us chugging along and on the rails. We don't have to do this alone. We have the Lord to rely on to show us the way. We just need to bear that sweet Fruit of the Spirit and follow Christ.

So, are you on the right track?

JULIA BETTENCOURT

ABOUT THE AUTHOR

Julia Bettencourt is the *lady* behind Creative Ladies Ministry, which she began as a website in 2001 to share ministry ideas for leaders involved in women's ministry in the local church. Her devotionals quickly became the number one reason that people visit her website. Over the years Julia has enjoyed sharing the little lessons that she's learned in everyday life through her writing.

Julia lives in California with her family. She and her husband have been married for almost 36 years. They have three children.

She no longer maintains the large CLM website that she did in the past. Julia is a long ways from when she started her website with two toddlers and a teenager at home. Her oldest child has now been married for nine years and both of her younger children are college students.

You can find Julia through her current blog where she shares what is on her heart and blogs about what is happening in her home life.

www.juliabettencourt.com